E. W. KENYON

T0001614

SIGNPOSTS
ON THE
ROAD TO
SUCCESS

FOLLOWING YOUR GOD-GIVEN PATH

WHITAKER
HOUSE

SIGNPOSTS ON THE ROAD TO SUCCESS
Following Your God-Given Path

Kenyon's Gospel Publishing Society
P.O. Box 973
Lynnwood, WA 98046-0973
www.kenyons.org

ISBN: 979-8-88769-126-8

Printed in the United States of America
© 2024 by Kenyon's Gospel Publishing Society

Whitaker House
1030 Hunt Valley Circle
New Kensington, PA 15068
www.whitakerhouse.com

Library of Congress Control Number: 2023952251

1 2 3 4 5 6 7 8 9 10 11 **W** 31 30 29 28 27 26 25 24

CONTENTS

INTRODUCTION

E. W. Kenyon gave talks on success during his regular radio program. His ministry received so many requests that they be put into book form that the result is this book that you hold in your hands, in the hopes that you can read, study, and learn the secret of success.

This book does not define the word *success*. That definition will be found in your heart.

Kenyon says, "God bless you. May these living messages lift you out of the commonplace life into the big, real life of happiness and success."

My spirit goes with thee
    Little book of my dreams,
Go waken the slumberer,
    Go strengthen the weak.
Encourage the disheartened,

> *To the lone dreamer speak, yes,*
> *Kindle within him a mighty desire,*
> *With dauntless ambition*
> *Set his spirit on fire.*

1

KEEP AT IT

"**H**ow did you ever do it? I can't see how anyone could do a thing like that."

We were in a curio shop. On the table there was a whole army of little figures that had been whittled out by hand.

What hours of work must have been spent on them. This friend of mine stood there, and looking at them said, "How did you ever do it?"

The man smiled and said, "I just kept at it."

I went out of the door.

I walked the street, and I heard those three words, "Kept at it, kept at it, kept at it." How they rang through my soul.

That man had "Kept at it." He had put life into it. He had made a success.

People were coming from all parts of the country to see the effect of that cultivated, trained genius.

All that man had done was to train his mind and hand, and then whittle his dreams out of wood, of soft stone and ivory.

I was thrilled through and through at the possibilities that were wrapped up in common folk like you and me.

I heard a girl play the piano. She was not over sixteen. I know something about music. We had a music department in our institution for many years.

I looked into her face and I whispered in my own heart, "Girl, you have spent hours pounding the keys while other girls were walking the street. While others were sleeping and mother was trying to get them out of bed, you were pounding those keys.

"You have lost a heap of good times, but what a musician you are!"

She kept at it. That is why she won.

I stood with a man, overlooking a beautiful farm in Northern Maine.

I said to him, "Who cleared this land? Who stumped it?"

He answered, "Do you see that little log house down there by the creek? I built that, and wife and I moved into it before there was an acre of this land cleared. I vowed that I would clear every acre of it and put it into crops, and I have done it."

That is the spirit that conquers.

"I vowed I would do it, and I have done it."

I stood by the loom in the factory as a boy and vowed that I would become an educator. I did not know what it meant, but I knew that within me was a teaching gift, an undeveloped thing.

I vowed I would do it. I did it.

I was handicapped as few men have been handicapped, but I did it.

I am passing it on to you to show that they cannot conquer you if you will to do it.

Struggle to improve. In every effort, improve the dream.

Every time you play that piece on the piano, play it better than you played it before.

Every time you sit down to that typewriter, make up your mind that you are going to be more efficient than you have ever been.

Make your brain work. It will sweat, but make it work. It will improve. It will develop until you become a wonder to those around you.

Don't depend on an alarm clock. Don't depend on mother's waking you.

Make up your mind that you will have the alarm clock in your soul.

Never depend on another man's car. Get one of your own. Be self-reliant.

Be punctual. Be diligent.

Think through on every problem.

Conquer your difficulties as a part of the day's job. We are out in the fight and we will win the crown.

2

WHAT HAVE YOU IN YOURSELF?

It is what you are, what you have in you, that counts.

It is the undeveloped resources in your mind, in your spirit, in that inward man that counts.

It is the developing of the writer, the thinker, the teacher, the inventor, the leader, or the business manager that is hidden deep in you that is important.

I venture that every one of you young men and women who read this have in you one of these abilities.

There may be an untrained voice, untrained musical abilities lying hidden under the careless, thoughtless exterior. Let us go down with a flashlight and look over the untouched treasures that are stored away inside, that have never been touched, never been used.

Then let us bring the thing up that we find and make it worthwhile and give it a commercial value.

For remember that everything that goes toward making you a success is inside of you.

The thing that makes opportunities, that makes money, that saves money, that creates new things, or that brings together things that others have created but were unable to utilize—this is inside of you.

Find it and make it work.

It is going to require a boss who is utterly heartless to rule over you. The boss is inside of you.

There is a slave driver in there whom you must bring out. Put the whip in his hand and tell him to go to it and make you a success.

There is something in you that can take these dreams of yours and make blueprints of them, and then can change the blueprints into buildings.

It is there.

That ability is there.

No one else can train it. No one else can develop it. Someone else may set it on fire, but you can quench the fire by refusing to act.

Remember that you must use the suggestions that come; you must rise up and put the thing over.

You must drive yourself, for no one else can do it.

Put yourself on a mental diet, not a diet of idle dreams nor idle fancies, but a diet of real mental work.

Be mentally awake and diligent. Put your best into every day.

Make up your day of saved moments and hours.

You are out to win. You are out to conquer. You can do it.

It would be different if this ability were in someone else and you were trying to awaken it.

It is all in you, and you are going to put it over.

3

USING WHAT IS IN YOU

There is a gold mine hidden in every life. Nature never made a failure. Every man has success hidden away in his soul. No one else can find it but himself.

He holds the key to the hidden room. Failure comes because we never sought that hidden treasure. Failure comes because we tried to find it somewhere else. You can't find it anywhere else.

Success, victory, and achievement are in you. The exceptional people are those who develop what is within them.

That quartet is winning fame and success because they developed what they had in them. Singly they could not do it but united, they make a harmony that thrills the heart.

The soloist had it in her. It was there, and she developed it and made it of commercial value.

I have seen three great baritones. One was a miner who would have been known the world over had he not been too lazy and loved the companionship of drinking men and useless women.

What a voice he had! I picked him up a drunkard. I tried to make a man of him. I bought him clothes. When it was known that Scotty was going to sing, the building could not hold the crowd.

I said to him, "I don't know whether my pianist can play the pieces that you want to sing without looking them over." He looked at me with a peculiar expression and said, "I need no accompaniment."

He stood by the piano that first night in his old mining clothes and sang. I closed my eyes, and I couldn't locate him because his voice utterly filled that whole room. He seemed to be everywhere in it. That great voice was strange, sweet, wonderful music. He made the songs all over that he sang that night.

I raised the money and sent him back to his own land. He promised to sing again. As a boy, he sang in Drewry but he confessed that he was so drunk, it took a man to hold him up. But he never amounted to anything. He did not develop the thing that was in him.

Genius has grown up to weeds about it, just because they did not develop the thing they had. I know it is hard work but you will learn to love hard work. There are no great gold nuggets lying on top of the earth now. You have to go down into the earth for them; you must dig for them.

You want the applause of the world? You want money to buy fine clothes and build splendid houses? Awaken, young men. Go find that hidden place in your own nature. Dig and dig until you have conquered.

A father was dying. He had two sons. The boys had always felt that he had gold that he had hidden away somewhere. He had never been a strong, healthy man, so his farm was not developed. In back of the house were ten acres of stump land. When he was dying, he said, "The stump lot." Again and again, he said, "The stump lot."

As soon as the funeral was over, the boys said, "The gold is out in the stump lot." How feverishly they worked! They tore up every inch of it. But they found no gold. Then the older one said, "We have the land in good condition. Let's put in corn." In the autumn, they found the gold in the ripened corn.

You have a stump lot in you. Dig it up, clean it up, and you will find the gold in it.

4

TRAIN YOURSELF

What you do for yourself counts far more than everything that others have done or can do for you.

Self-discipline is the most important feature in any life.

Unless you put yourself under mental discipline, you will never develop the forces in you that are valuable to the commercial world.

Rule your temper so that no matter what happens, what is said or done, your temper will be under absolute control.

The man who does not rule his temper can never achieve the success that belongs to him.

He destroys the building that he erects.

Govern your tongue, so that it will say nothing that will injure anyone around you.

Practically all the injury that is done to a character, a business, a home, or a person is done with words.

It is tongue work.

The man or woman who makes no contribution to destructive thought and talk is a valuable asset anywhere.

He is deaf to anything that is destructive to another. He is blind to anything that folks around him do.

He cannot speak of it. He has mastery of himself.

The efficiency of an office force is reduced sometimes 50 percent by idle, unkind words.

The man who can govern his temper, his tongue, and his appetite, though he has but mediocre ability, is bound to get to the top.

Gaining the mastery of these will be among your first real victories.

It is controlled power that is valuable.

That waterfall is simply beautiful. It has no commercial value until it is harnessed.

It is the harnessed ability in you that is worthwhile, ability under intelligent mastery.

Find out what you wish to be or do, then train yourself for it.

What you have undeveloped in you has no value. No one else either wishes or has the time to develop it. That is your business.

The training is all done by you.

If you have a voice, put yourself under a teacher, then work and carry out the teacher's instructions.

If it is art, put yourself under a competent instructor and obey the laws of art and work.

Nothing will take the place of hard work, intelligently directed. Talents in you need push and determination to make them worth money.

It is you, and you alone, who will do the developing.

The lazy person who waits for something to turn up is a failure.

The only things that will turn up are overdue rent and other bills. Nothing will take the place of self-denial and hard work.

It is easy to become a failure; all you need to do is to idly dream.

It is the man who wills and keeps on willing who wins. Don't float. Don't wait for an opportunity. Go make your opportunity.

Put your whole self into life. Study and drive yourself. Always remember that your worst enemy is inside of you.

No circumstance and no person or combination of persons can conquer you as long as you do not destroy your own prospects yourself.

Don't be satisfied with anything you do. Always seek to improve yourself.

5

WHAT ARE YOU WORTH?

What value do you place on yourself?

Have you ever taken an inventory, or have you just said, "Well, I know I could do it if I would. I believe I can sing better than that person who is singing now." Or, "I believe I could build a business." Or, "I could be this, or I could be that."

Are you going to be what you *could* be?

Honestly, are you worth anything in your own estimation? Have you set a price on yourself?

Have you set a price on your own ability, on your own time?

What is your word worth to you?

When you say, "I will get that lesson," or "I will conquer that subject," or "I will master that problem," is your word worth anything? Do you make your word come true when you say, "I will give that up; I will put that thing over?"

What is that word worth to you? Have you faith in your own word?

I am not asking what your word is worth outside.

Pride may make you keep your word with people, but do you keep your word with yourself?

You are too valuable to barter away the finest part of manhood or womanhood—your word.

You are worth more to yourself, most likely, than to anyone else, but by a year from now, can you make yourself so valuable that men will pay any price for you?

Great corporations are looking for men and women who can earn fifty thousand dollars a year.

Set your mark—your standard—high. Then go up there. Allow no day to go by in which you have not improved yourself.

Take an inventory again and again and see what you possess. See whether that possession is more valuable today than it was a year ago.

Find where your ability lies. Then put all of your best into that ability and make that ability come across and put you over.

Remember that what you have hungered and yearned to do, you have the ability to do—if you will.

6

WHY ARE YOU A SPIRITUAL FAILURE?

Modern preaching has produced the modern spiritual failure that we see in the church.

Failures are not ready-made; they are the product of the teaching that we have had or the absence of the right teaching.

I am convinced that most people will come to the level of the Father's purpose if they know how.

The spiritual failure I am talking about is one who is born of God but who has never developed, who has remained in an infant state through many years because of malnutrition. They feed upon the theories of men rather than upon the Word of God.

They have lived in the realm of sense knowledge, rather than in the realm of the Word of God.

They are ever praying for faith, not realizing that all things belong to them, that God has *"blessed us with every spiritual blessing in the heavenly places in Christ"* (Ephesians 1:3), and that at the very beginning, God marked us out for adoption as sons and daughters through Jesus Christ. (See verse 5.)

You see, the purpose of the Father was healthy, vigorous children.

Can you conceive of an intelligent earthly parent who wishes to give birth to children who will be sickly, half-witted, deformed creatures? Why, the thing doesn't sound reasonable.

And do you think the heavenly Father takes pleasure in having us mentally, physically, and spiritually sick?

Do you think Jesus likes to contemplate the number of Christians who are in hospitals, undergoing hideous operations and going through the torture of the damned?

7

ALL HAVE ABILITY

I did not believe this once.

I thought that there were but a few who had real ability, and that the rest of us belonged to the mob.

I venture to say that it will be almost impossible to pick out a single person in any large establishment who does not have the ability along some line that could make him outstanding if it were developed.

I am dictating this little article for the ambitious man or woman—not for the man who is too lazy to develop what is in him, but for the man who is unsatisfied with anything but the best.

As I study men and women, I am convinced of this: There are very few who have developed the possibilities within them to the limit.

There is no overdevelopment.

Many people are in the wrong place in life.

They have no gift for the thing they are trying to do. They are doing it simply to get by.

There is room and a salary waiting for the man who has ability and is willing to put hard work into it.

Choose your work rather than having the work in which you have no interest thrust upon you.

Find out what you can do, what you like best to do.

I don't care who you are. I don't care what your handicaps are. They have never made a handicap that could hold any man down who had in him the yeast to rise.

Most of the people who are at the bottom are at the bottom because they will to stay there. That is where they belong.

It is a hard thing to say, but it is true. I am now what I willed to be through all these years.

The first thing to do is to find out what you want. Set your eyes on the goal. Then fight for it.

There must be an objective.

When you find that objective, set your compass and sail for that star.

8

PUTTING YOURSELF IN THE
WAY OF SUCCESS

If only I could repeat it over and over again, so that wherever you turned in this book, your eyes would see this one fact: You have within you all of the qualities and elements that are necessary to make you a success. Your chief work is the development of the thing that nature has already given you.

Before you go to the office, create all around you and in you an atmosphere of victory.

You go out with the consciousness that you have victory. You and the unseen One are going down to the office together and you are going to put it over.

You are going out after that job with the smile of a victor— not the smile of a man who is trying to smile, but the man who smiles in spite of himself.

Cultivate the habit of thorough work. If it is mental work, think every problem through. Be the one man in that office where you work who thinks through on every problem that comes up.

You will find that the boss will want you.

Very few men have the ability to think through. They guess, they speculate, or they theorize.

But down yonder behind the desk is the man who takes the problem and resolutely drives himself to think through that problem from every angle.

The boss can get men to do what he tells them to do.

He is looking for one with ability to tell the others how to do it.

So set the standard high for yourself. Have a lofty spiritual ideal.

Climb to it.

Between you and it, there may be many a swamp through which a road must be made.

Lumbermen always build roads to the timber they wish to market.

You will have to build a road to market your abilities.

There is pain and fatigue ahead for you, but you dress for the job.

Remember to associate with people who have won, those who help you climb to the top.

Don't hang around with a group of *has-beens*. Associate with the men who are climbing up.

The idle, gossiping people will not help you. The lazy and careless will stand in your way.

Those who spend their nights in the roadhouse or at the gambling hall will never help you.

Don't think you can get something for nothing. Put your money where it will count.

Put your time where it will pay you dividends.

This battle is not for the thoughtless, heedless guesser or idealistic dreamer.

It is for the man who works.

THE HAPPY SPIRIT

The glad smile from an honest heart is better than a sermon.

A smiling salesman has the deal half made. You can sell more easily with a gracious smile than you can with a dead, unresponsive countenance.

Mothers who start the day with kindness, smiles, and tender words have happier homes.

The fathers who try it will make the breakfast a glad half-hour.

It is the key that unlocks so many hearts.

We wish to remember the glad face, the happy smile, and the joyful words.

We want to forget the other kind. Tones are better when we smile.

The voice is richer when smiles are blended in it.

A smiling clerk or a smiling salesman is the one who attracts us.

HOW WE WIN

Reason makes the plans.

The strong one carries them through. The strong one is your will.

Dream, then carry out your dreams. Drive yourself to the finish line.

The will-less dreamer is never a success.

You have the vision. Make it come to pass.

You dream your dream, and then make the dream come true.

Cultivate a discontent with everything that is common in yourself.

Compel yourself to improve your mind and your natural abilities.

If you have the gift of cooking, be the best cook in the community.

If you have a gift, no matter what it is, make that gift stand out until men will admire it.

Then someone will want to pay the price for it.

A young man had an unusual gift for dressing windows. He had worked in a store for a long time. He had watched the window dresser and given him suggestions until, by and by, the window dresser asked that he might become his helper.

It was but a few weeks until the helper became the artist. The head dresser never told the boss who did the art work, but men came from different parts of the city to look at the windows.

There was always a crowd in front of the store.

One day, a man came from a distance. He asked who dressed the window. The manager introduced him to the head dresser.

The man was disappointed. He said, "He does not talk like one who could do this kind of work."

The young man had stood by. Later, he was introduced.

The man said, "Do you dress these windows?" The young fellow said, "I am only the sidekick."

"I have this amount of space in my window," the other said. "What would you do with it?"

The young man said, "If you will come back this afternoon, I will tell you."

He went into his office and drew the plans. When the man came back and looked at it, he said, "I will give you twenty-five hundred dollars a year if you will go back with me."

The young man had been working for fifteen dollars a week.

You cannot hide trained genius. You cannot hide trained ability.

Other people may use you for a time, but you will break the bonds sooner or later like this young man did.

It is in you. Pull it out.

IT IS THE YOU IN YOU THAT WINS

Peter speaks of *"the hidden man of the heart"* (1 Peter 3:4).

That is the *You* that is in you.

The visible you is not the You who puts you over. It is the unseen You who wins the fight.

The *seen you* may be very attractive or very repellent.

It is the unseen You with whom we really wish to become acquainted.

It is the unseen You, this hidden man of the heart, who runs the whole machinery, who is the boss of the institution.

He is the man who is to build you into success.

He is the fellow who raises the money to put you over.

He is the one who made the *seen you* come across and make good.

It is this unseen You to whom I am writing. I am trying to reach him and cause him to make the *seen you* study, work, and make yourself worthwhile in life's game.

It is the unseen You who makes the *seen you* worthwhile and makes you do things that have commercial value, who makes you do things that the world is waiting to have done.

I am saying to the unseen You, "Get behind this *seen you*. Make him work. Make him study. Make him dig until he has won the fight."

WHAT'S THE USE?

God has forgotten me, and nobody cares. I might as well throw up the sponge."

These words were said to me just a few weeks ago by a young woman.

I asked her how she knew that God had forgotten her and how she knew that nobody believed in her.

She said, "I have had nothing but failure ever since I came to the city."

I said, "Don't you think we should take an inventory and find out why you have had failure? What is the reason for it? When a person has a string of bad luck, I feel like diagnosing the case and, if possible, finding what is wrong."

"Well," she said, "I was whipped when I came. This was the frontier of last resort to me. I was simply running away from bad luck in the East."

I said, "You didn't expect to win, did you?"

She said, "I had hoped I might. I thought if I could get in the right surroundings, I might get on top."

But I noticed a hopeless strain in her voice and a look of hopelessness in her eyes.

I said, "Let's go back to the beginning of things for a bit. You know that God cannot fail anyone who trusts Him. Suppose you bring Him your shattered, broken present. Then make a new start today. He will wipe out all the past, and as He wipes it out, you begin now as though you had never tried and failed."

She said, "Oh, I would give anything if I could do that."

"But you can do it," I said. "All those who have reached the top have had to do it. Many of the dreams and expectations of youth have been lost.

"But there have been born new dreams and new expectations. The faith of youth and young manhood and womanhood has been destroyed, and a new faith has been born out of the failures of the past."

I can see her now. "If I could only do that," she said. "If there could only be born in my heart a new faith, a new dream."

I said, "Your worst enemy is your memory. Your worst trait is going back over the failures and taunting yourself. You cry nearly every night after you go to bed because you have failed."

She said, "Yes, that's true."

"But," I said. "You are done with that. You are done with all that is past. Failure is a memory thing to be forgotten. Right now, we are writing on a new page, a new history. You have a new name. The name is Victory. We will call it Victoria. We will christen this new girl with a new name, and you will go out to win.

"You can succeed. Life is big and rich ahead of you. Let Him, the Unseen One, take care of you."

She whispered softly, "Do you think He would do it?"

"I know He would. He counts it a privilege. He is looking for opportunities like this. I imagine He has had His eye on you for a long time, waiting for you to look up through the clouds and ask for His help."

She went out to win.

I met her days afterwards.

She had no past. She had nothing but a brilliant, glad future ahead of her.

She said, "You know, it was so easy to get a job. I went in to the same store where they had turned me down, and they seemed to be glad I came. I am doing the work I enjoy."

Those of you who are chasing after a better job have in you the possibilities of a better job.

Don't spoil them. Sell yourself to the man who needs you.

It is easy to do it when you have the right mental attitude toward life.

13

LOOSE TALKING

Careless speaking is a vicious habit.

When one realizes that his words are the coin of his kingdom, and that his words can be a cursing influence or a blessing, he will learn to value the gift of speech.

Control your tongue, or it will control you.

You will often hear men say, "I speak my mind."

That is well if you have a good mind, but if your mind is poisoned, it is not good.

An idle word spoken may fall into the soil of someone's heart and poison his whole life.

What a blessing good conversation is, and what a curse its opposite.

Make your tongue a blessing, never a curse. A person is judged by his speech.

Your words make you a blessing or a curse. Your words may carry a fortune in them.

Learn to be master of your conversation.

14

HANDICAPS

There are few who have reached the top who have not been handicapped.

Obstacles stand in the way of the man who climbs.

I don't know why this is, but I know it is true.

These obstacles have to be overcome, but in the overcoming, one fits himself for places of responsibility.

I thank God for poverty, for need of self-denial, for self-culture, for long hours of study and hard work.

The inward drive to plod on when tired is the thing that makes men strong, self-reliant conquerors.

Every failure stimulates them to harder work. There is no giving up.

There is no yielding. Facing impossible circumstances becomes a daily experience to the conqueror.

He learns to win. He has cultivated the will to win, the will to conquer.

He kept the fires of ambition burning. He has made work a part of himself.

He has a group of very fine habits. He has the habit of study, the habit of control of his eyes and ears, the control of his passions and ambitions.

He is master.

He is the man who uses the public library and secondhand book stores.

He is ever studying to improve himself in his place. He knows his trade, his business, his profession.

He makes himself an authority in his particular field. He counts his handicaps a blessing.

He goes on with God and wins.

No man is a failure until he lies down and the undertaker puts him under the sod.

15

THE WRONG SLANT

It is no use. I might as well give it up. Every time I try, I only fail. Every job I get, I lose. Every dollar I get ahead, something happens, and I have to use it. I am no farther ahead now than I was ten years ago. There is something dead wrong somewhere."

I said to him, "Friend, what has been the difficulty?"

He said, "I don't know."

I said, "I will tell you what your trouble is the way it appears to me. You have the wrong slant on life. You have talked about your failing, your difficulties, until they have become a mental disease.

"I venture to say that the last man of whom you sought to find employment read you like a book and said, 'I don't want that man in my crew. He is a chronic fault finder.' You have had so much trouble that you have eaten it, slept with it, and dreamed it until it oozes out of you."

He said, "I know it, but how can I overcome it?"

I said, "It is the easiest thing in the world to overcome. Solomon's solution was to, *'Trust in the* LORD *with all your heart, and lean not on your own understanding'* (Proverbs 3:5 NKJV). In other words, go into partnership with God, where you cannot fail."

He said, "But that is religion."

"There is no religion about this. You are dead wrong. Religion is a man-made thing. This is a God-made thing. This is common sense to link up with God. You take Jesus Christ as your Savior, and you confess Him as your Lord. The moment you do, you receive God's life and ability, and you cannot fail. If you will walk with Him, you can no more fail than Jesus failed."

"But Jesus failed on the cross, didn't He?"

"Yes, but it was the greatest victory which came out of that failure that has ever been known. That was divine strategy. He will make you a conqueror if you walk with Him."

FACING LIFE AS IT IS

Don't say, "If things were different, I would do something."

Do something with things as they are.

Facing your life as it is now and winning is the object.

When things go hard and money stops coming in, or you lose your job and everything goes wrong, take account of stock. See what is wrong. See what you have forgotten, and go on and conquer.

We dream what we would do if…

Now wipe out the *if*.

Dream and do it regardless of circumstances.

You say, "That cannot be done."

It *can* be done. There is no *can't* about it.

The man who wills to do it—who puts up the fight and is willing to do the work—can put it over.

A young man discovered a vein of gold high up in the mountain.

He needed power. He needed money. He needed to know how to develop it. He struggled and worked and failed.

Sitting down one night after a long hard day, tired clear through and through, he said to himself, "I know where my difficulty is. I don't know anything about this rock. I don't know anything about geology, and I know nothing about mining. I am going down to the city and find out."

He came down to the city, went to the head of the mining department at the university, and laid the case before him. The professor called up a mining engineer. He met the young man. The young man told his story.

The engineer said that he must go and see the vein. It took about a week to get there.

After the engineer had seen it, he said, "There are millions there. But it will cost a great deal to get in there and develop it. You will have to organize a stock company or sell it. Which will you do?"

The young man said, "I am going to develop it."

It took him a year of hard training and study. He gave himself utterly to it.

Through the long winter months, he drove himself until he had acquired the knowledge that he needed when the springtime came.

It made him millions.

The trouble with too many people is that they want to get it too easily.

Most of us say, "If I had a chance…but circumstances were against me. I don't have an education. I didn't have the pull."

We lay our failure to the lack of opportunity.

The other fellow, handicapped worse than we, made opportunities.

He fought until opportunities came to him.

Success belongs to the man who simply wills to do it. He is the man who makes success come his way.

The fellow who lies down and says, "I can't do it" is a failure.

Never lose heart because the first efforts fail. Go back and find the reason.

Pick up the wreckage of old failures and build them into success.

You can do it.

17

JUST A WORD OF WARNING

Children's lives are largely made up of words—the words of their parents and those whom they love and admire.

A mother can fill her boy's heart with zeal for an education and a position in life, or she can, with words, destroy the finest spirit that was ever given to a home.

The children are word-made.

What do I mean?

Their lives are made up of words of their parents and loved ones.

The wife little appreciates the power of words on her husband's life. When he loses his job, she could scold him and tell him that he is no good. He was whipped before he came home, but he would then be doubly whipped.

Instead, she puts her arms around him and says, "That's all right, dear. You will get a better position. You are worthy of a better job anyway."

He goes out the next morning thrilled by the touch of her lips and her words, which have filled him with courage and confidence.

He leaves her heart filled with joy and gladness, and she says, "What a man God gave me."

He says, "What a woman you gave me, Lord."

They have learned the secret of words.

A few devastating words could have filled his mind with confusion, his heart with pain, and his eyes with tears.

Words give heartache, and words give strength, comfort, and faith.

Let's be careful of the words we use.

Don't tell that story you heard the other day about this man or that woman.

Don't let any other ears be poisoned as your ears have been poisoned with it.

Never repeat scandal. Never repeat the calamity. Let others do the talking about that.

You keep your lips for beautiful things, helpful things, comforting things.

That is your job.

18

THE MENTAL HITCHHIKER

Are the fish worth the cost of pole, line, and hooks?

Is honor and competence in old age worth saving, self-denial, and hard work in youth?

Would it not be better to spend your money and squander your time, knowing that when old age comes, there will be a pension of fifteen or twenty dollars a month?

These are suggestions that face earnest young people today.

You can spend your time in the roadhouse, in the shows or dances, or idly roaming the streets; or you can drive yourself to study and fit yourself for the place that is waiting.

Everywhere, big business is hunting for competent help.

Many mediocre men fill places of importance because no one can be found who is really fitted for the job.

It is surprising how difficult it is to find even a good stenographer, to find someone who can take charge of a department

49

and make it a success, to find someone who will take a vital interest in the work and put it over.

Almost every man and woman is a time server.

His ambition is to get his wages with as little work as possible.

The new mental attitude is to get without giving.

You cannot be a success and do that.

The good old days of honest labor seem to be but a dream today.

The road that leads to a good bank account is an uphill road, and most of us have to build the road ourselves.

The hitchhikers are filling the road today. They want someone else's car to ride in. They want someone to buy the gas. They want someone to pay the taxes and give them free passage.

Are you a mental hitchhiker? Are you a mental hobo?

Or are you one of the fellows who pay the taxes, build the roads, and bear the burdens?

If you are a success, you will have to bear the burdens. You will have to pay the taxes for a hundred other people. The easy way is to hobo it.

It is the way of least resistance.

I believe a fellow can get used to going on short rations, wearing old clothes, and sleeping in the jungle, but as for me, I am going to go to the top.

I am sending out this invitation for the rest of you to come with me.

19

LOYALTY

Everyone who employs help places loyalty above almost any other trait in his help.

We need skilled mechanics. We need skilled workmen in every department. Regardless of their skill, if they are disloyal, they hinder production. They hinder efficiency, and they hinder the growth of the business.

The new class consciousness that has been developed in the last few years along political lines has been of great injury to our nation.

What we need is old-fashioned loyalty to the man or the company for whom we are working.

The spirit of loyalty gives a sense of security to the firm. It is a guarantee of a higher grade of production, of a higher quality of the thing produced.

It guarantees permanency and safety in investment.

No one has a right to draw a salary from a firm if he will not be loyal to the firm.

If one cannot be loyal, he should find another position.

The first thing that we expect in a man, after efficiency in his trade, is loyalty to the company.

It should be taught in our schools and in our homes that we are not rendering to the firm or company our best until we give our heart's loyalty in our service.

20

WHAT ARE YOU GOING TO DO?

What of life?

You are standing on the threshold. Before you lie the untried paths.

What are you going to do?

Have you chosen your work, your vocation, and your place in life, or are you drifting, hoping that something will turn up?

It will, but the thing that turns up will be of no value to you unless you are ready to take it as it comes.

Don't float. Dead fish float.

Make up your mind that you will put your dreams into a blueprint and then, with that blueprint in hand, you will build your mansion.

Find your place, but be sure that you do thorough preparatory work.

Put real hard work into the days of preparation.

Don't just get by. Don't be satisfied with anything but 100 percent plus. Fight for it. Work for it. Enjoy it. Make it a game to win.

Be a success in youth, and you will be a success in middle life. You will be crowned in old age.

Make yourself a wanted person. Be so valuable that if you had to move, men and women would weep because of your departure.

If you plan to be a minister, be God's best. If you go into business, be the best in your community.

If you plan to be a lawyer or a physician, put a trained, cultured personality into it.

Whatever you do, plan to build your house on top of the hill.

Harness that lazy mind and make it work.

That mind can make a place for you.

Let me say again to you, "Go under your own steam."

Prepare yourself, and doors will open to you everywhere.

21

THE BELL RINGER

You are selling from house to house. You are ringing bells.

That is a good place to start life. I started it there.

You meet a different person every five minutes.

If you can get them to listen to you, that is the first step. So many simply say, "I haven't time," and then slam the door in your face. You smile and go to the next. That's the game.

But the man who can get inside the house to display his goods is the man who puts it over.

The first requisite is a smile and a glad, "Good morning." It is not an ingratiating smile, but a wholesome, big, warm smile.

You know you have something that they need, something they ought to have.

You come there with the heart of a philanthropist. You have something to give.

They are going to get something worth more than they pay for it.

You are not trying to outdo them, but you are there to give them something worthwhile.

I didn't know anything about the sales game when I went into it as a boy of twenty-one.

Salesmanship was not taught then as it is today.

I became one of the pioneers of sales talk, teaching the art of salesmanship.

But I found that I could not sell unless I had confidence in the thing I was selling.

I was selling pianos and organs from house to house.

I tried to sell an instrument in which I had no confidence.

I was an utter failure.

I went back to the office and asked the manager which was the best piano for such a price.

He told me. I went to the factory to find out all about pianos.

I wanted to know how the things were built.

I went through the factory and studied them until I knew everything a young fellow could learn about the instruments.

Then I went out on the road.

I knew that I had the best thing on the market for the money.

I knew that if I could get a piano into a house and get the boys and girls to practice, it would change the future of that home.

I went out to help the community. I succeeded.

It was so easy to sell when I had the right mental attitude toward the people.

I was trying to bless them.

I was trying to help the folk who bought. Do you see the point?

That is the real art of salesmanship. I was so dead in earnest about it.

I was so enthusiastic about the bargain that I had that I carried them off their feet.

I sold to people who had no music in them. I sold to them because of the excessive, burning desire in my heart to make them happy.

That is the thing which sells.

Settle it in your own mind. Is the thing you are selling worthwhile?

If it is not, then get something that is.

If you are selling insurance, bonds, autos, or groceries, know this: If your entire ambition is simply to get the money out of it, you will fail. But if you are giving them something that is going to be a blessing, and you are enthusiastic over it, you will be a success.

THE CHRONIC KNOCKER

Nothing hurts a firm more than to have in its employ men holding important positions who are chronic knockers, who are always finding fault with the business, with the management, or with the material they use.

Men of this type should be eliminated.

One man of that kind in a church will wreck it. One man of that type in a crew of men in the lumber camp will cause the entire organization to disintegrate.

Chronic knockers will spoil an organization and wreck its prospects.

Men who talk too much and talk unwisely are a detriment to any organization.

Never knock your firm.

Never knock the goods you are selling because you are selling yourself in every deal. The man who knocks the firm for which he works knocks himself because he is there.

If he is not satisfied with it, he should get out and go somewhere else.

We have no right to stir up strife and bitterness while we are drawing a salary from a firm.

We have come to an unhappy place.

We have been taught politically to hate the people who have been successful in life, that if a man has gained a position of affluence, he must be bad.

That is wrong.

Men like Henry Ford have climbed to the place they occupy by sheer efficiency and downright honesty.

Class hatred is an unfortunate thing.

It does not belong in a democracy. It does not belong anywhere.

Why should I hate the man who is smarter than I am and who has achieved more than I have?

I should honor him and thank God that there are men of that kind.

Class hatred robs a nation of its efficiency; it robs men of the pleasure and joy of fellowshipping and working with each other.

There should be a notice put up in every factory, store, and shop that reads, "No knockers are needed. We need boosters.

We need helpers. We need men who encourage, not men who discourage."

Make up your mind that whatever you say will be constructive.

Just knocking for the sake of knocking is ignorance gone on a rampage.

23

BE WORTH MORE THAN YOUR SALARY

Put the company for which you work under obligation to you.

Keep society under obligation to you.

The world's greatest scientists, chemists, and mechanics have all put the world in debt to them.

Be a real contributor to your age. Don't just exist.

Mothers, give to the world some great sons and daughters. Put your best into their training.

You have no idea how dependent the world is upon mothers.

Make the world a better place because you lived in it and played your part.

Selfishness cramps ability.

Be bigger than the blunders that you make.

Live big. Be big in your dreams, in all things that you do. Learn to love men.

Only lovers count.

Give to the world better service with every added year.

Forgive your enemies. Never go to their level and hate with them. The lying and opposition of your enemies is your diploma.

Give a heaping measure in all your ministry.

God is the original giver. Be in His class.

24

THREE THINGS THAT BREAK US

These are mental traits that can be conquered.

The *first enemy* is putting off decisions and action until a later period, never deciding anything when a decision is demanded.

You face a great crisis in your life. You know you ought to make yourself mentally proficient along a certain branch of study.

You are filled with enthusiasm…until you take up the books. Then you say, "I'll start this tomorrow."

The moment you say that, you are defeated. Usually, one might just as well throw his books into the fire because tomorrow, he will repeat himself.

The secret of winning is action.

A *second enemy* is mental laziness. This is widespread.

It is the line of least resistance and can be cured only by the sternest methods.

The You that is in you is the real master of your mental processes. The You that is in you is the You the world is seeking.

You must so honor that You that you give it its place of authority and dominion over your faculties.

Now drive your mind to work. You absolutely refuse to give it any rest until it has accomplished the desired amount of work.

You must be absolute master of yourself, of your faculties, for your mind will always be lazy until interest has been created. Then it flows on smoothly.

A third enemy is wrong talking, negative talking.

I knew a man who started out in business with every promise of success. He had the right location. He had the right kind of business. He had a multitude of friends. He was a good buyer and a good salesman.

I went into his store on my way to the post office nearly every morning.

I used to admire his store. It was so clean. The details were so carefully managed.

A change came over him.

He had a little domestic difficulty. He began to talk discouragingly.

In two years, that man talked himself out of a splendid, growing business.

I did not know then what I know now, or I could have stopped him.

He simply talked himself out.

He discouraged people who came in. He was full of pessimism and doubt. He challenged everything.

Finally, he talked himself into absolute failure.

You cannot afford to talk failure, doubt, or fear.

Why? Because words register in your heart and after they have registered, they take control of your life.

25

DEVELOP YOUR RESOURCES

Most of us are like wild land, undeveloped.

We show signs of real wealth, but it is lying underneath the roots and stumps and refuse that need to be cleared away to make the soil usable.

Here is a voice with marvelous timbre, but no training. They write across it, "Unusable, undeveloped."

Here is a face with a smile that has wrapped up in it a fortune, but the mind behind it is untrained, unfit, and unready. We write across it, "Unavailable."

What we need is hard work—not work on impulse, but on principle. We need to drive ourselves until we have developed the rich resources within us.

The time to do it is now.

Begin today to clean up that rich bottom land in your nature and get it into production at once.

Make everything swing into line now to the one great objective of your life.

Determine your future; settle what you are going to do and then make every day pay tribute.

Form habits of study, habits of industry.

Learn to save the moments; the hours will take care of themselves.

Form the habit of concentration, downright hard thinking. Drive your mind. Become an absolute slave driver over your own faculties. They are your slaves, your servants.

Make them work. Make them study. Make them develop. Kill laziness and that droning habit of dreaming.

Transform it into vital energy.

Set the dynamo of a tremendous purpose loose inside of you.

Indecision and wastefulness of ability and time must be destroyed.

Fight for time. It is the most valuable asset you have.

Cut every corner. Save every moment.

Be exact with yourself. Put yourself on a schedule. Make yourself do your best.

Wasting time is wasting ability. It is wasting the thing that makes you worthwhile.

Learn to use it. Make your time your wealth. Make moments pay dividends.

Carve out of every day that which spells success for tomorrow.

Make yourself worthwhile. Make people want you.

Make yourself so attractive, so vitally attractive and so valuable that men will hunt after you.

Make opportunities where no opportunities ever existed before.

Make yourself ready for the opportunity.

26

ALL HE HAD WAS WORDS

This is a little study of great things.

One man started out in life without sponsors, without a university education, and without money. Someone said to him, "What have you besides your two hands to make a success of life?"

He said softly, "I have nothing but words."

The friend smiled, not understanding him.

So he started on his lonely quest for success with nothing but words.

He learned the secret of putting things into words, of making words living things.

He freighted his words with clear thought, and after a bit, he learned the secret of putting his fine, clean, splendid manhood into his words.

Men began to set a value upon his words.

People would stop him on the street to engage him in conversation just to hear his words.

You understand that almost every man who has climbed to the top of the ladder of success has climbed with words. Here and there, a man has climbed because of an unusual voice or an unusual gift of artistry, but the majority of men have gotten their feet on the first rung of the ladder of success by words. They climbed rung by rung to the top.

A man must put a valuation on his own words before others will sense their value.

The ambitious man's words became his bank account. He studied, he dug deep, and he thought through on problems.

Other people learned to trust his judgment and his words, rather than to study for themselves.

There is a vast army of people who have certain business ability, but they have to hire others to do most of their thinking.

He supplied that want. He did the thinking.

By and by, they were willing to pay him almost any price to have him think for them.

His words became valuable. They were his servants. How they labored for him!

He filled words with inspiration, comfort, and hope for others.

He sent them out on wings until they passed from house to house, from lip to lip. He found himself being quoted here and there.

His words were doing things.

They were his servants working for him. He had learned the secret of words.

By and by, publishers paid him almost unthinkable prices for his words.

Why? Because he had learned the art of filling words with inspiration and new life.

Let's study words.

Let's learn to fill them with goodies for the children, healing for the sick, and victory for the discouraged.

We will win.

27

BY YOUR WORDS

Perhaps they never told you, but they measure you by your words.

You are rated by your words.

Your salary is gauged by the value of your words.

Your words make a place for you in the business in which you are engaged.

Neither jealousy nor fear can keep you from climbing to the top if your words have value that belongs at the top.

The organization is bound to give you the place that belongs to you if your words bring forth the right results.

You don't have to put on airs and you don't have to exaggerate. All you have to do is to be natural, but make that *natural* worth listening to.

Study your work. Study how to say things. Study how to use words that will change circumstances around you.

Make an analytical study of words, then see how much you can put into a single sentence.

I don't mean how many words, but how much you can put into the words so that when men and women listen to your words, they will be thrilled by them.

The store clerk said, "Good morning" in such a way that I turned to look at her.

She had put something into her words. She had put herself, her personality, into her words. Her words rang.

She sold me some pencils, but she sold them as though she were selling a car.

After I had left the store, I felt inclined to go back and watch her deal with other customers.

Cut out the useless words that stand in the way.

Eliminate all the words that would hinder the thing you want to put over from reaching the mark.

Make your words work in the hearts of those who listen. Trust in words. Trust in the words of your own lips.

Fill them with loving truth.

Think in your heart of how you want to help those who are to be your customers, how you are going to bless them, and how the thing that you have is necessary to their enjoyment.

It is what you put into your words that makes them live in the hearts of the hearers.

Empty words die in no man's land.

They never get over the trench. If they do, they are duds.

If they do get across and people hear them, they amount to nothing. Living words—words bursting with heart messages—thrill and grip.

Love always seeks the right word to convey its message without loss in transit.

Clothe your thoughts in the most beautiful words, but don't sacrifice pungency for beauty. Blend them.

28

PUTTING YOUR BEST INTO WORDS

Empty words hold no more interest than last year's bird's nest.

When we fill the words with ourselves and we are honest, our words will be honest.

Others grow to depend on them.

I know a young man whose words are filled with love, unselfishness, and a desire to help people. Whenever he speaks in the company of people, they listen to him.

Nowhere do words have the strange effect that they do in a radio message.

The minister who speaks over the air in a cold, dead voice will get a cold, dead response. No matter how beautiful the thoughts he has or how beautifully he clothes them, if the words are not filled with love and faith, they don't live.

Faith is built by words.

Deeds have their place, but deeds are the children of words, in a large measure.

You speak, then I watch you perform. It is your speech that attracts my attention.

Your deeds have their place, and we give you credit for them, but it is your words that set us on fire.

You can fill your words with anything you wish.

You can fill them with fear until the very air around you vibrates with doubt, fear, and restlessness.

You can fill your words with fear germs, and you fill me with fear of disease and disaster.

Your words are filled with interrogation points, with a sense of lack, hunger, and want…

Or you come to me and your words are filled with faith. Your faith words stir me to the very depths.

I wonder why I ever doubted.

Your words enwrap me within themselves.

Your words are like sunlight, like coming into a warm room from a cold frosty atmosphere outside.

Your words pick up my drooping, broken spirit and fill it with confidence with which to go out and fight again.

They are faith words, wonderful words.

The reason Jesus's words had such far-reaching influence was that they were faith words.

When He said to the sea, *"Peace, be still"* (Mark 4:39), the very sea grew quiet, and the winds hushed their noise to hear the words of faith from the lips of the Man.

The deaf could hear His faith words. The lame and broken could rise and walk and run because of His faith words.

There was something in His words that drove disease and pain out of the body and fear out of the heart.

I can hear John say, "I used exactly the same words, and that boy was not healed. Now the Master takes the words out of my lips and fills them with something, and when they are heard, the child is healed."

What did Jesus put into His words that had such healing power?

A salesman is talking. He says, "I cannot understand it. I used the same argument, the same method, and I utterly failed. I used almost the identical words, and yet they said, 'No, I cannot buy today. I have no special interest in this thing.' Then the other man came and took my seat. He used the same formula that I had. The man became interested immediately.

"After a while, he reached into his pocket and pulled out his checkbook. What did that man have that I didn't?"

One man's words were filled with pure mentality. He said the things like a recording. The other put living faith, interest, and love into his words.

When this last salesman sat down, there was a look of quiet assurance on his face, and his first sentence registered because he believed in the thing he was selling.

He not only believed in it, but he believed that if the customer purchased it, it would be a blessing to him.

It was a safe and wise investment.

This man generated faith, created faith in the customer.

The customer put his hand in his pocket and held it there quite a while. He was holding onto his checkbook. By and by, he said, "I will take so many shares. That looks good to me."

His check was written and signed. The deal was made.

Why? Because the salesman had filled his words with faith.

29

STEPPING OUT

Stepping out of sin-consciousness into son-consciousness is stepping out of failure into success.

It means stepping out of that inferiority complex that has held us prisoners for years.

It means becoming the thing you have dreamed.

Do you remember the picture in the magazine of the little scrawny fellow sitting by the side of a great, big, strong, muscular man, seeing the big man take his girl away from him? Then the little scrawny man goes into the gymnasium and develops his muscles until they are strong. Then he goes out and faces other men unafraid.

You go into God's gymnasium and come in contact with the great gymnastic teacher of spiritual things. You let Him put you through a course until you stand in front of the world complete in all His finished work, until your inferiority has been swallowed up in His dominant victorious Spirit, until you whisper, *"Greater is he that is in* [me] *than he that is in the world*" (1 John 4:4), or "Greater is He than the doubts and fears that worked in me in the past."

I have a Master now who is building me up instead of the master who kept me in bondage, who kept me down.

I walked in failure for years. I walked with the sense of my lack of ability and righteousness, but now I walk with Him. We are linked together. I am breathing in the courage of His tremendous personality. I am filled with His ability.

I say goodbye to the dark, unhappy days of the past. A curtain falls between them and me. I stand now upon the highlands, a victor.

No longer am I worrying about the lack of money. Lack of money does not lord it over me. I am master.

Lack of ability does not lord it over me now. Lack of opportunity no longer lords it over me.

I am not intimidated by circumstances or filled with fear that I cannot do the work or put it over.

I know that the Mighty One has taken me over and is putting me over since I stepped out of sin-consciousness into son-consciousness.

30

DON'T BREAK ME WITH WORDS!

This was Job's cry to his friends. (See Job 19:2.)

They came as comforters. They stayed as tormentors.

Words heal, and words break; words destroy, and words make life as we find it today.

Words heal us, and words make us ill. Words bless us, and words curse us.

The words I just heard will linger through the day.

How little women realize that a biting, stinging word in the morning will rob her husband of efficiency through a whole day.

A loving, tender, beautiful word, a little prayer word, will fill him with music that will lead him on to victory.

We need the martial music of faith that only our loved ones can give to us.

How little we have appreciated the tremendous power of words—written words, spoken words, and words set to music.

A Southern officer said to a Northern friend, "Had we had your songs, we would have conquered you."

A political speaker said, "You won the election because you had better speakers than we. We had more money but we did not have words well spoken."

You see, men and women, that a study in words is one of the most valuable assets in a life.

Learn how to make words work for you. Learn to make words burn.

Learn to fill words with power that cannot be resisted. Mussolini held Italy in his hand by the power of his words. Austria was conquered by Hitler with words—no powder, no poison gas, no bayonets—just words.

How we wait for a message made up of words.

The secret of advancement in life lies in the ability to say the right kind of words.

My ministry over the air is a ministry of words.

I fill them with love; I take God to fill them with Himself, and so I send them out to bless and cheer.

Mothers, your home atmosphere is a product of words.

Your boy failed because wrong words were spoken, right words were not spoken.

Why is it that some families grow up so clean and strong, fight their way through college, and go out in life's fight and win?

It is because the right kind of words were spoken in the home.

Words make a boy love education.

Words bring a boy to church or keep him away.

Think of something of infinite importance and then learn to choose the right words to express it.

Then send the words out with pen or tongue. The way we say it has tremendous weight.

Every public speaker should make a study of words, the kind of words that count.

Then before he leaves his study, he should so charge his mind with God and God's ability that when he stands before the people, that ability will fill his words until his people are thrilled.

He should make the delivery of words a study, an art.

He should fill all his words with kindness, with love. Every man in the sales game should make himself a master of words.

Try out words in your own home. See how they work.

Fill your lips with lovely words, beautiful words, until men will love to meet you, long to hear you speak.

Remember, words are apples of gold in network of silver.

WORRY DESTROYS EFFICIENCY

Worry is the unhealthy child of fear and unbelief. Those two are married—and what children they have begotten!

Worry leads to the wasting of vital energy, the disturbing of the digestive system and other organs, which impairs your ability.

It becomes a mental disease. Almost everyone has it. It is contagious. It leads to all kinds of physical and mental disorders.

Its cure is simple: *"Trust in the LORD with all your heart, and lean not on your own understanding. In all your ways acknowledge Him, and He shall direct your paths"* (Proverbs 3:5–6 NKJV).

Or, *"Casting all your anxiety upon him, because he careth for you"* (1 Peter 5:7).

Get quiet for a moment and remember this: God is on your side.

If God is for you, who can be against you? (See Romans 8:31.)

They can't conquer the man who trusts in the Lord with all his heart.

There aren't enough enemies in all the world to whip the man who trusts absolutely in the wisdom of God his Father and does not lean upon sense knowledge.

No man is safe to go out into the business world until he has first learned the secret of absolute trust in the Lord.

So if you haven't learned it yet and you are bearing your burdens with fretting, care, and anxiety, go alone and settle the great issue with Him.

Take His wisdom and grace to go out and do your work with perfect efficiency.

32

GIVE YOUR BEST

Today's opportunities perish with the setting of the sun. While the sun still shines, it is a challenge to your heart.

The world is waiting for you.

It waited for Caruso. It waited for Nordica. The world waited for Henry Ford and Woolworth.

You have something in you for which they have been searching.

No one can rob you of it. No one can defraud you of it. You have it in the safety vault of your own being.

There is a better day coming—a glad, rich, wonderful day—and you will have a share in using that day.

So get ready for your big moment, your opportunity. In these days of opportunity, of preparation, put your best into every effort of your life.

Be big in your thought life.

Prepare yourself to reign as a king somewhere in some realm.

Your best will give you life's best, for you understand that we draw interest only on what we have deposited.

Life gives us dividends for our investment.

Give your best to every task. Get the habit of doing fine work. Make each job better than the last.

Fear to slight your work for the habit will grow on you. The most trustworthy man becomes untrustworthy then. You cannot play with duty.

Get the habit of making each deed a finished product. That carries with it an invitation to get acquainted with its Creator.

33

CAN IT BE GUARANTEED?

Can everyone be successful?

The fear of failure hangs like a dark cloud over many lives.

I know that success belongs to everyone of us.

We may not be great financiers or great authors, but in our place in life, we may know that we have won.

It is necessary that we make the right choice, find out what our talents and abilities are, and have them properly trained and fitted to achieve the desired end.

There are a few things that are absolutely imperative if we are to fulfill our part of life's program.

There must be a purpose from which we cannot be swerved.

There must be the right kind of companionship. The wrong kind of associates are a serious handicap, but it can be overcome.

Some of us will be handicapped with physical environments that seem almost insuperable, but we can conquer.

A young man came to me just recently to talk over his future. He said, "So far, I have been a failure."

After he opened his heart to me, I saw where his difficulty lay. What he needed was God's help and companionship. I am not talking religion—for I never talk that—but this young man needed the help that only He, the great unseen One, can give.

He said, "Will you tell me just how to get in contact with God?"

He was genuine. That young man was real. My heart went out to him. There was something so big, so full of the right kind of ambition, that he challenged all that was in me.

I said to him, "It is necessary that you take Jesus Christ as your Savior and that you confess Him before your family, before the world, as your Lord."

He looked up at me and said, "That should not be difficult. No one should be ashamed of Him."

I said, "The moment you do it, God will give you eternal life. You will become His very own child. Then you will not only have the help of God as your own Father, but you will have the intercession and strength of Christ.

"Then He will give you the Holy Spirit, who will come into your life and live in you. You will soon find what this will mean. You can do a great deal alone, but when you have received eternal life within your spirit, that will increase your intellectual efficiency 10 to 50 percent.

"As your mind is renewed through reading the Word, you will find a freshness in life such as you have never known. You will know that God is in you, that His ability is your ability."

"You can face any kind of a problem now and know that you are a victor. Your words will have something in them that they never had before. There will be a power in your very presence that men will feel.

"Always give God His place. Give Him a chance to show Himself. I don't mean that you are to talk religion to people. You just let God have His place in your life, and you will talk about Him. You will know that He is in you. You cannot fail with Him in you."

Nay in all these things, you are more than a success.

You can do all things through Him who gives you strength.

These mighty Scriptures—Romans 8:37 and Philippians 4:13—will hold you. God will be the strength of your life. He will make Jesus to be wisdom to you.

That new, strange, wonderful, love nature of God will permeate your very being.

You will be wanted. Men want genuine men and women around them.

You will have the thing the world needs and the world lacks.

You will find your place in life easily with this new addition of wisdom, strength, and ability in you.

CONCLUSION

You have read it. You have felt the thrill of new ambition tugging strongly at your heart.

Now what are you going to do? Are you going to let it end with just a thrill, or are you going to begin now to make life worthwhile?

You have been stimulated. You have been lifted. Now go to work.

In each page you'll find me hiding,

I'll be living when I'm dead,

I'll be firing your ambition

When these living words are read.

ABOUT THE AUTHOR

Dr. E. W. Kenyon (1867–1948) was born in Saratoga County, New York. At age nineteen, he preached his first sermon. He pastored several churches in New England and founded the Bethel Bible Institute in Spencer, Massachusetts. This school later became the Providence Bible Institute when it was relocated to Providence, Rhode Island.

Kenyon served as an evangelist for over twenty years. In 1931, he became a pioneer in Christian radio on the Pacific Coast with his show *Kenyon's Church of the Air*, for which he earned the moniker "The Faith Builder." He also began the New Covenant Baptist Church in Seattle.

In addition to his pastoral and radio ministries, Kenyon wrote extensively. Among his books are the Bible courses *The Bible in the Light of Our Redemption: From Genesis Through Revelation* and *Studies in the Deeper Life: A Scriptural Study of Great Christian Truths*, and more than twenty other works, including *The New Kind of Love*, *The Father and His Family*,

Jesus the Healer, In His Presence: The Secret of Prayer, The Blood Covenant, and *Two Kinds of Righteousness.*

His words and works live on through Kenyon's Gospel Publishing Society. Please visit www.kenyons.org for more information.